501 Ways to Boost Your Child's Success in School

Robert D. Ramsey, Ed.D.

author of *501 Ways to Boost Your Child's Self-Esteem*

Library of Congress Cataloging-in-Publication Data

Ramsey, Robert D.
   501 ways to boost your child's success in school / Robert
D. Ramsey.
      p.   cm.
   ISBN 0-8092-2548-4
   1. Education—Parent participation—Handbooks,
manuals, etc.   2. Home and school—Handbooks, manuals,
etc.   I. Title: Five hundred one ways to boost your child's
success in school.   II. Title: Five hundred and one ways to
boost your child's success in school.
LB1048.5.R36   2000
371.19'2—dc21   99-53466
                                                     CIP

Cover design by Monica Baziuk
Cover and interior illustrations copyright © EyeWire, Inc.
Interior design by Susan H. Hartman

Published by Contemporary Books
A division of NTC/Contemporary Publishing Group, Inc.
4255 West Touhy Avenue
Lincolnwood (Chicago), Illinois 60712-1975 U.S.A.
Printed in the United States of America
International Standard Book Number: 0-8092-2548-4
00 01 02 03 04 05 LB 14 13 12 11 10 9 8 7 6 5 4 3 2 1

Contents

Introduction

All parents want to give their children the help, support, and encouragement necessary to achieve and excel in school, but too often parents don't know what to do or how to do it. At last, here is a powerful collection of user-friendly, school-tested ideas that can help every parent give his or her child an academic edge.

When students don't make the grade in school, it's frequently the parents who have failed. Not by choice, but by default. What teachers and administrators know that others don't is that parents make all the difference when they know how to set their children up for success. This guide shows the way.

501 Ways to Boost Your Child's Success in School is a pocket-size guide crammed with quick tips, insider information, and practical advice. Each page reveals new insights about what teachers like and look for, what pushes their hot buttons, how schools really work, what it takes for students of all ages and abilities to succeed, and how parents can help.

This is the first fingertip sourcebook to spell out practical suggestions all families can use to increase the odds that their children will succeed in school. It contains strong medicine in capsule form for curing student fears, phobias, and failures in school.

501 Ways to Boost Your Child's Success in School covers many topics not normally included in most parent guides. School success isn't just about brains, good study habits, and hard work. It's also about attitude, assertiveness, timing,

politics, positioning, relationships, getting noticed, self-confidence, pro-social behavior, and, most of all, parental involvement. Finally, these topics and more are presented so parents can use them to their children's advantage.

None of the many books for parents on schools and schooling are as down-to-earth, easy to read, and simple to apply as *501 Ways to Boost Your Child's Success in School*. This isn't a text on educational theory. It's simply a jargon-free collection of hard-hitting advice that can work for any student or any parent in any school.

This guide differs from others in many ways. It's short, practical, fun, easy to read, and hard to forget. Digging deeper than most traditional, politically correct parent handbooks, this guide probes topics not found in other guides, such as

- insider tips for getting along with teachers
- what they don't tell you in the school handbook
- how to survive a bad teacher
- the "proper art of bitching" to school personnel
- what to do if your child thinks school "sucks"

The commonsense suggestions apply to all age groups, subject areas, and school situations. All this and it fits in a pocket or purse. How intimidating can that be?

Your child deserves success in school. You can help make it happen. Let *501 Ways to Boost Your Child's Success in School* release the good student inside your child. Reading this guide may be the most important homework assignment you ever had. And there's no test on Friday.

An Overview of School Success

1.

School success is learnable. You start
by believing that all students can learn
to study better, retain more, maximize
their natural strengths, work the system
to their advantage, and position themselves for success. If you and your
child don't believe this, it won't happen.
If you do believe it, you're well on your
way to school success. Reading this
book can help.

2.

Helping your child succeed in school is
often a matter of "more or less":

- Listen more, lecture less.
- Question more, nag less.
- Praise more, nitpick less.
- Seek suggestions more,
  give advice less.

3.

School success is a decision. You and your child must make it together.

4.

Love your children too much to allow them to be anything less than their best.

5.

To succeed in school today, kids need what they have always needed: structure, discipline, challenges, respect, recognition, chances, choices, second chances, amnesty, and tough love. Finding ways to meet these needs is what parenting is all about.

6.

Set high expectations. They can transform any barrier. Assume success and it can become a self-fulfilling prophecy.

7.

Don't expect all As, no matter how bright your child is. Rigid and unrealistic expectations cause children to feel they have to earn parental love by living up to impossible standards. Your job is to help your children *be themselves*. That's the way they'll learn the best.

8.

Be realistic about school successes. Expect problems. Expect solutions. You won't be disappointed on either count.

9.

If you miss a sale or a deal falls apart at work, it doesn't make you a bad person. If your child goofs up at school, the same rule applies. Expect success, but accept human limitations and bad luck.

10.

Always accept best effort as success.

11.

School success is a family affair. No student can do it alone. Make sure everyone does his or her part.

12.

Don't let others define your child's potential.

13.

School success is a worthwhile goal. Perfectionism isn't. Don't be too hard on your child or on yourself. Give each other permission to be imperfect.

14.

If you want to take credit for your child's successes in school, accept some blame for any failures as well.

15.

You can't buy school success. Don't pay your child for doing schoolwork. It won't produce a better student, only a spoiled brat.

16.

Don't ask for or expect any favors for
your child. Students grow stronger by
getting things done on their own, not by
having things done for them.

17.

Don't praise mediocrity. Praise for
praise's sake cheapens real achievement.
Praise effort and genuine accomplishments. Praising anything less is a false
promise.

18.

In all you do to boost your child's
school success, try to be a model
more than a critic.

19.

Sometimes, the best way to help your child succeed is simply to be available to listen.

20.

Through all the daily ups and downs, keep your child's long-term educational goals in mind. It helps to have a star to follow.

21.

When things fall apart at school, remember that your child isn't bad, lazy, or stupid—just young!

22.

Your children can have the education you want for them. It may take hard work, extra effort, tough choices, sacrifices, and assertiveness, but it can happen. If it doesn't, some teachers and administrators may be at fault—but the real reason will be that you and your child didn't want it badly enough.

2

Getting Your Child Ready to Succeed

23.

Start early. The brain connections your child makes soon after birth (and even before) help determine school success later on. Expose your child to many different stimuli from day one. It's never too early (or too late) to begin giving your child an edge.

24.

Help your child build a bank of varied background experiences. Broad experiences give kids more reference points for understanding the world and making meaningful connections. Students with a rich repertoire of firsthand experiences learn quicker and more easily.

25.

Buy activity toys that help develop
coordination and improve motor skills,
and creative toys that stimulate self-
expression. Toys can be learning tools.
Garage sales are a good, inexpensive
source.

26.

Always welcome questions and never
penalize curiosity.

27.

Research shows that children who do
well in school have at least one caring,
competent adult in their lives who values
education and pro-social behavior. That's
you. Be there!

28.

Understand that children learn through play. Encourage creative free-play time. It's the way kids rehearse for school and for life.

29.

Establish routines. They work wonders. Kids thrive on structure.

30.

Involve your children in situations where they experience a "cycle of success":

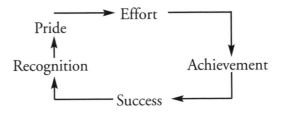

31.

Notice when your child improves.

32.

Allow mistakes without guilt or shame.
As Zig Zigler says, "Failure is an event,
not a person."

33.

Expose your child to nature. It's life's
greatest teacher.

34.

In your family, make it OK to make
mistakes, try and fail, or have a bad idea.
Without this permission, your child can't
risk enough to succeed.

35.

Don't expect consistency, logic, unselfishness, or other miracles from your child.

36.

Set appropriate boundaries and consequences. It's the key to raising good kids and successful students.

37.

Show your child positive ways to calm down.

38.

Never belittle your children's imaginations or stifle their dreams. Kids who dream big achieve more.

39.

Challenge your child's mind by asking lots of open-ended questions. All children can learn higher-level thinking skills. They just need practice.

40.

All successful learners have a positive self-image. They believe they're "enough." Help your children's self-esteem:

- Show your love.
- Expect them to do their best, not be the best.
- Honor each child's special abilities.
- Spend time with each of them.
  For more suggestions, read
501 Ways to Boost Your Child's Self-Esteem (Contemporary Books).

41.

When friends come to play with your preschooler, use a timer to teach taking turns. They will need this skill to get along in school later on.

42.

Start and end each day with comfortable rituals. Kids need anchors to stay focused and reduce stress.

43.

Encourage divergent thinking by asking trigger questions such as "Is there another way to do it?" or "What else can you think of?"

44.

Model civility. Kids can learn it.
Teachers love it. Society needs
more of it.

45.

When reading to your preschool
children, you will more likely whet their
appetites for reading on their own if you

- get comfy (reading should "feel
  good")
- use verbal sound effects and
  different voices to enliven what
  you read
- relate each story to familiar life
  experiences

46.

Give your children some responsibility at home. They'll like it and become accustomed to it. Better yet, the results will carry over to their schoolwork later on.

47.

Model a positive view of the future. Hope keeps kids (and adults) going when things get tough. Pessimists make poor learners and poor leaders.

48.

Chase your child's interests. Every interest is an invitation to new learning.

49.

Praise and encourage your young children's "pretend writing" (scribbling). It's another way to support their interest in learning how to read.

50.

Read to your child—a lot. It's not just a cliché. It works. Children whose parents regularly read to them learn to read earlier, easier, faster, and better than other kids.

51.

Stress vocabulary building early on. Words are power. Make sure you give your children this power so they can succeed.

52.

Dealing with diversity and getting along with all kinds of people are learned skills that are essential to school and life success. As a parent, face your own prejudices. How you treat people who are different teaches your children a powerful lesson.

53.

When talking to preschoolers about the letters of the alphabet, use the sounds (not just the names) of the letters. It will boost your child's beginning reading. That's what phonics is all about.

54.

Model good relationships at home. It helps kids learn to get along with others. "Getting along" is one of the secrets of school success.

55.

Don't try to force a "leftie" to become a "rightie." You'll only frustrate the child and yourself. Left-handedness is OK in schools today.

56.

Give your child lots of choices. It teaches decision making and problem solving.

57.

Help develop a nurturing neighborhood that puts children first. Research shows that a caring neighborhood helps kids succeed in school and reduces the frequency of negative, dangerous, or at-risk behaviors.

58.

Looking for an activity that promotes fitness, improves coordination and grace of movement, boosts confidence, instills mental toughness, and teaches self-discipline? Try karate.

59.

As you read or view action stories with your child, talk about what the characters must be feeling or thinking about. Boys and girls need to learn that violence, explosions, and car crashes are scary, hurtful, and can seriously harm people's lives. Discussing these issues helps develop a more sensitive, empathetic, and caring child. Most successful students have these traits.

60.

To help little learners recognize letters and their sounds, try having them trace the letters in sand with their fingers while saying the sounds. Tactile learning works with kids of all ages.

61.

When checking out a prospective school, look for signs of excitement, laughter, fun, and pride. Students' faces can tell you a lot more than a parent handbook ever will.

62.

Never judge a school from the curb. It's what's going on inside that counts.

63.

If you can learn only one thing about a school you are considering for your child, learn about the principal. Good principals make good teaching and learning possible.

64.

Don't take everything you read in the school's handbook or prospectus at face value. As Charles Sykes wrote in *Dumbing Down Our Kids* (St. Martin's Press), "If you want to know what is really important to a school, don't ask the principal; look to see if spelling and grammar are corrected on a child's paper."

65.

Pick a school that isn't run for the convenience of adults.

66.

Hold a dress rehearsal to prepare your child for the first day of elementary school, middle school, and high school.

67.

Don't be afraid to use some undercover ways to size up a school.

- Talk to custodians and bus drivers. They know what's really going on.
- Look for graffiti and other gang signs.
- Check on the number of police calls to the school.
- Listen to how the office secretary treats people and responds to inquiries.

68.

Consider delaying school entrance if your child (especially a boy) lags in socialization skills, maturation, or skill development. A year's delay may give your child an added edge in being able to cope and compete.

69.

Readiness doesn't just happen. Work with your child to ensure proper preparation for starting school. Most kids can name colors, recognize the letters of the alphabet, and count to twenty or more before the first day of kindergarten. Early skills are linked to later academic performance.

70.

If you want to help your child learn to print the letters of the alphabet, start with the capital letters like the schools do. Teachers begin with uppercase letters for a reason. Uppercase letters are stick figures with mostly straight lines, while lowercase letters have lots of curves, squiggles, and loops, which are harder for little hands to make.

71.

Make a big fuss about buying school supplies and clothes with your child. This shows that going to school is a special event.

72.

Write an encouraging sidewalk message in chalk to your child on the first day of school. It shows how special the day is.

73.

Break down career stereotypes. Not all scientists are weird old men in lab coats. Not all nurses are female. The more options that remain open, the more excited your child will be to learn what it takes to choose the right one.

74.

Most schools provide a list of essential school supplies (e.g., pencils, scissors), but smart parents know that the "basics" also include Kleenex, house key, emergency phone numbers, identification, and telephone change. Make up your own unauthorized list of basic school supplies.

75.

Make a big deal out of your child's first day of school. Be upbeat, but calm. Skip the horror stories from your youth. Don't get weepy. Let your child choose what to wear and take a comfort toy along. Be sure, of course, to videotape the event.

76.

To help ease your child's separation anxiety on the first day of kindergarten, hide your own anxiety, explain everything in advance, say good-bye without making a scene, and leave without vacillating. Make a big deal out of pickup time, complete with smiles, hugs, and a treat. Kids quickly figure out that they can't have a happy pickup time without a drop-off time.

77.

When your child goes off to school, be sure you know the teacher's name, the principal's name, the school phone number, bus routes, and emergency closing procedures. You never know when you'll need this information.

78.

Encourage your child to develop a checklist for getting ready for school. Using a checklist teaches organization and reduces the need for nagging.

79.

Pay attention to your children's appearance. Help them look their best every day. If they feel good about what they wear and how they look, they'll do better in school. Adults dress for success. Why can't kids do the same?

80.

Get your child a library card. It's a passport to the latest information and the best literature in the world.

81.

Nurture your child's individuality, but also do what you can to help your child fit in with the other kids (e.g., similar clothes, same style of backpack). It will make your child more comfortable and more readily accepted by classmates. This makes learning easier, too.

82.

Start your child on the computer as early as possible. Kindergarten isn't too early. (In fact, it's a bit late.) If you don't have a computer, bring one home from work; check out a laptop from your library or school; or access computers available in public libraries, school media centers, or community center computer labs.

83.

Get your kids their own magazine subscriptions. This helps start a lifelong habit of regular reading.

84.

Make it a family tradition to give your children at least one learning gift (e.g., book, magazine subscription, science kit, educational toy, software) for each birthday. Such a tradition underscores the value you place on knowledge.

85.

Museums aren't just for grown-ups. Kids can learn a lot of science, art, and history in museums, too. Take your children often. It's another way to give them an edge.

86.

Provide your child with at-home opportunities for sharing possessions, helping others, solving problems, teaching cooperation, and making friends. This helps reinforce the school's efforts to teach social development.

87.

Let your children see you reading and studying at home. It makes learning seem normal.

88.

Do whatever it takes to help your child nail down the basics in the primary grades. Keeping up is easier than catching up. Students who start out right usually end up all right.

89.

Make grocery shopping a learning experience. It's a good opportunity for kids to learn about weights and measures, counting change, and other math skills. They just might also turn out to be smarter consumers in the process.

90.

Everywhere you turn, there are opportunities for your children to hone their beginning reading skills. Use them all, including cereal boxes, baseball or trading cards, and crayons that name their own colors.

91.

Remember Robert Fulghum's bestseller, *All I Really Need to Know I Learned in Kindergarten*? Here's some of what Fulghum learned in the "sandbox at Sunday School":

- Share everything.
- Play fair.
- Learn some and think some and draw and paint and sing and dance and play and work every day some.

Be sure your child learns these lessons in kindergarten and at home.

92.

Learn the age-appropriate behaviors for students your child's age. Despite the wide variations, a general idea will help you have more-realistic expectations of your child's school performance.

93.

When they're old enough, try to expose your children to a variety of adventures (e.g., snorkeling, rock climbing, white-water rafting). They will learn responsible risk taking—a necessary ingredient for exceptional achievement.

94.

Thoughtful conversation promotes learning. Have real discussions with your children about real issues. Respect and value their ideas and opinions. It will make them stronger students and yours a stronger family.

3

Keeping
Learners
Safe and
Healthy

95.

No school can be perfectly safe, but some are a lot safer than others. Do whatever you can to place your child in a safe school. Transfer your child or move if you have to. There is no school success when fear occupies a seat in the classroom.

96.

Give your student the latest street-smart advice for staying safe in today's world, including the following:

- If you feel threatened, run to a woman for help. (Women are less likely to be predators and more likely to listen to a little child.)
- Be leery of strangers asking for directions or help finding a lost pet.
- Trust your feelings.

97.

The safer the school, the better your child will learn. Here are four ways you can help:

1. Lobby for more community policing in school zones.

2. Request that local firefighters (who are on duty but not out on a fire call) be visible where kids are going to and from school.

3. Identify one "safe home" in each block where children can go for help in an emergency.

4. Urge neighbors to turn on yard lights when winter days are shorter and children come home from school in twilight or early darkness.

98.

Make friends with a good pediatrician. Good health and school success work together. Sometimes when problems arise at school, a change in diet or a pair of glasses is all it takes to get learning back on track.

99.

Provide an adult presence at school bus stops during times of loading and unloading. A good day at school begins and ends at a safe bus stop.

100.

Have a secret code word that must be given by anyone picking up your child from school. Precaution is part of doing business as a family today.

101.

Threatened kids can't learn. Never downplay or ignore the seriousness of a bully's threat. The bullied child knows the danger is real and has a right to expect the parent to help.

102.

Send healthy snacks with your child on important test days. They may provide just the boost your child needs to score well.

103.

Stress frequent hand-washing. It won't make your child any smarter, but it can reduce illnesses and absences. Better attendance usually means higher achievement and better grades.

104.

Train your children to cover up their own coughs and sneezes and to stay out of the way when others are spreading germs. Kids exchange more colds and viruses at school than they do notes.

105.

Head lice are nasty and ugly. They love schoolchildren and spread faster than rumors. The good news is they aren't necessarily signs of uncleanness and they're not life-threatening. If your child comes home with head lice, just follow the school's directions: scrub, disinfect, wrap up toys, and keep your child home until the lice are gone. Lice won't hurt your child's learning unless you make your child feel embarrassed or ashamed about getting them.

106.

Respect the school nurse or health aide.
If the nurse calls to say your child needs
to come home from school, he or she is
trying to protect your child, not mess up
your day. Be glad your children have a
caring health partner at school.

107.

Wheaties has it right. Champions do eat
breakfast. Research shows that kids who
eat breakfast have higher grades, better
attendance, less depression, less anxiety,
and are less likely to be hyperactive. Be
sure your champions eat right every
morning.

108.

Don't send your sick children to school just because they don't want too many absences on their record. They may end up missing more than would have been necessary if they had stayed home in the first place.

109.

Lock up your guns and ask the parents of your child's friends to do the same. Children who are victims of fatal shooting accidents will never know school success.

110.

Always take the gateway drugs (tobacco and alcohol) seriously.

111.

Put together an identification (ID) folder for each of your children. Include a recent picture, a fingerprint, and any other distinguishing information. In the case of a disappearance, an ID folder can be an invaluable tool for the police. Preparing for the worst isn't paranoid anymore.

112.

Pay special attention to the dangerous downtime between school dismissal and the parents' return from work. This is when kids are most likely to get into trouble. Get your child off the streets and into supervised learning or recreational activities after school.

113.

Watch your child's weight. America has an epidemic of obese children today. Unfortunately, overweight kids get teased more, have lower self-esteem, do worse in school, and have more health problems than other children. Kids don't get fat by themselves— parents help. Show your children how to make healthy nutritional choices. They'll feel better and do better.

114.

Many American schools have air-quality problems today. Find out if your school has had a recent safe-air evaluation. If not, join with other parents to insist that one be conducted. Kids can't do their best when every day is a bad-air day.

115.

Make sure your child understands that reporting the presence of guns or other weapons in the school isn't squealing or being a snitch or tattletale. It's called *survival*.

116.

If your child is frequently too tired to go to school, don't let it slide. Arrange for a physical checkup. If there appears to be no medical basis, know that depression or low self-esteem can often cause fatigue in students. Check these out, too.

117.

Help your child see the connection between healthy living and effective learning.

118.

Train your children to watch what they eat during the schoolday. It can affect their performance for several hours afterward. For maximum mental alertness, limit caloric intake.

119.

Dare to talk to your child about drugs and alcohol early on. The middle-school years may be too late. If you don't talk about these subjects, plenty of others on the street will. Let your example speak loudest of all. Drugs and school don't mix.

120.

If your child is still worn-out Monday morning from losing sleep at Saturday night's sleep-over, put "overnights" on hold until vacation time. Setting limits is the only way to set your child up for success.

121.

Establish and enforce a regular bedtime. Well-rested students learn better.

122.

Establish a curfew. Curfews are part of the structure that supports school success. Your child will squeal at first, but will be glad in the long run. You'll both get a lot more sleep as well.

123.

Alarm clocks aren't just for waking up. Teach your children to set one to remind them when it's time to go to bed as well. Rest and routine are prerequisites for school success.

124.

Arrange for your child to learn
conflict resolution techniques
such as active listening, brain-
storming solutions, and reaching
compromises. The ability to settle
disputes peacefully can keep your
child safe from confrontations and
make it easier for him or her to
concentrate on studies.

4

Parents as
Teachers

125.

Remember that you are your child's first, foremost, and favorite teacher. Ask yourself "What kind of teacher am I? Am I teaching the right things? How can I do better?"

126.

Teach your child values. They are the cornerstones of achievement. Start by teaching
- respect for others
- respect for self
- respect for property
- being responsible

127.

Teach your child to check for accuracy— every time.

128.

Teach your child how to listen by
modeling good listening skills yourself.
Kids need to learn that real listening is a
lot more than just waiting quietly for
your turn to talk.

129.

Teach your children first *how* to learn
and worry later about *what* they will
learn.

130.

Model curiosity, discovery, and a sense of
wonder. Keep trying new things. When
parents are lifelong learners, kids are
more apt to take learning seriously.

131.

Teach your child manners. Courtesy still counts in the classroom. Being polite doesn't take brains, money, or good looks, but it can give any student an edge. Teachers are biased toward the well-mannered child.

132.

Teach your child to break big tasks into smaller ones. It's a survival skill in and outside of school.

133.

To develop responsible students, model responsible behavior yourself. It's 11 P.M.—do your children know where you are?

134.

Children can be taught to be optimistic and to expect success, but these subjects aren't taught in school. That's your job.

135.

Teach your child that, in your family, failure is temporary.

136.

Teach your children the power of first impressions. Teachers make snap judgments just like everyone else.

137.

Teach your children to set priorities.
It's the only way they can deal with
today's countless demands on their
time and attention.

138.

Teach your children to stretch—to strive
to do more than they think they can.
Challenge them to keep trying and not
to settle for what's comfortable.

139.

Teach your child the power of a good
start. Part of winning is getting a jump
start on others.

140.

Help your child develop resilience. School won't be all successes. There will be some disappointments. Self-confidence, optimism, a sense of humor, and family support can give your child the ability to bounce back and overcome bad events.

141.

Teach your children that they, not their teachers, choose what they learn.

142.

Teach your child a simple formula for studying. Second- and third-graders aren't too young to learn the classic SQ3R approach: survey, question, read, recite, and review.

143.

Teach your child that one way to
get the right answers is to ask the right
questions. Successful learners know that
the only stupid questions are the ones
unasked.

144.

Teach your child to plan ahead.
(What else is there to plan for?)

145.

Teach your child to respond to setbacks
with renewed effort. Second effort is a
key to success.

146.

Teach your child to associate with winners. Success can be contagious.

147.

Teach your child the power of goal-setting. It's a survival skill that can change your child's life.

148.

Teach your child to get noticed in positive ways (e.g., by being prepared, volunteering, sitting up front, asking good questions, and helping out). Getting noticed is always a step toward better grades.

149.

Teach your kids to make the most of mistakes. Finding out what went wrong and correcting mistakes is a powerful way to review and master material. Mistakes are tools when they're used correctly.

150.

Teach your child to use humor or clever verbal responses, such as "Get a life," to lighten up tense situations with other students. Anything that makes school life go more smoothly makes learning easier.

151.

Teach your child to paraphrase what they hear. This technique sharpens listening skills and confirms comprehension.

152.

Teach your children to practice damage control by apologizing and making amends if they've been disrespectful to a teacher.

153.

When they're old enough, teach your kids that no single accomplishment lasts forever. Without continued learning, today's success is only a memory waiting to happen.

154.

Teach your children to pace themselves. When tackling schoolwork, the best students work as quickly as they can, but as slowly as they need to.

155.

Teach your children to believe in "plan B." Winners always have a backup strategy.

156.

Successful students set goals. Help your children by teaching them the popular SMART model for goal-setting. It's simple: all goals should be specific, measurable, action-oriented, realistic, and time-based.

157.

Teach your child to use positive affirmations to build self-confidence. It's one way kids can talk themselves into school success.

158.

Teach your child to slow down and take time to think. The best critical thinkers don't rush.

159.

Teach your child that the best way to learn to write well is to read good writing.

160.

Teach your child that some questions have more than one right answer. (The next step is to convince teachers of this.)

161.

Minutia matters. Train your child to pay attention to the little things that can make a difference (e.g., name on all papers; all pages numbered, in order, and stapled if necessary).

162.

Teach your children to practice visualizing. It's a form of mental rehearsal. What they can visualize, they can achieve.

163.

To prepare your children for the world of work, teach them the seven things all employers want: (1) responsible behavior; (2) timeliness; (3) the ability to get along with others; (4) effective communication; (5) problem-solving skills; (6) ability to follow through; and (7) willingness to accept feedback. Surprise! The exact same traits are needed for school success.

5

Working with Teachers, Administrators, and "The System"

164.

Schools work only when the home-school partnership works. You will almost always get out of school what you put in. Do your part.

165.

Base your choice of a public, private, or parochial school for your child on personal and family values. If you want religious training for your child's everyday education, the public schools can't deliver it. Only the public schools, however, can offer exposure to the diversity that reflects the real world. As a parent, you have to make the call.

166.

Don't complain about the school not doing its job until you're sure you have fulfilled all your responsibilities to the school, including the following:

- Be sure your child attends regularly.
- Inform the school of all absences.
- Inform the school of important family changes.
- Inform teachers of your child's special needs.
- Be available and accessible.
- Keep informed about what's going on at school.
- Support the school's discipline policy.

167.

Know what the best schools are like. Even if you don't have a choice, it pays to know what makes a winning school. If nothing else, you will gain a vision of what your school can become—with your help.

168.

Know what's available from the school. Your child can't benefit from special programs and services if you don't know about them.

169.

Communicate regularly with the school. No news isn't necessarily good news. It may just mean you don't know what's going on.

170.

You don't have to love, or even like, your child's teachers, but you do have to work together. It's easier if you understand what makes teachers tick, such as

- Most teachers feel overworked and underpaid.
- Teachers don't like to criticize other teachers.
- Teachers aren't always prepared. (Who is?)
- Some teachers feel more confident around kids than around adults.
- Some teachers are uncomfortable with volunteers in their classrooms.
- Most teachers blame parents for many of the school's problems.
- Teachers gossip like everyone else.
- Teachers have long memories.

171.

If your child has special needs, be sure to alert the school early on. The earlier special needs are spotted, the easier they are to meet. The best time to start working on problems is now.

172.

Never hesitate to request the school programs, classes, teachers, and services you feel strongly about.

173.

Meet your child's teacher(s) and exchange phone numbers early on. Kids act differently and work harder when they realize their parents and teachers know each other.

174.

Learn how to talk to teachers:
- Catch them during downtime.
- Be polite.
- Listen.
- Stick to facts.
- Ask for clarification.
- Agree to do your part.
- Allow time for their solutions to take hold.

175.

Insist on plain talk from teachers. Only insecure professionals hide behind jargon.

176.

Never let anyone define your child by an IQ or any other test score.

177.

Realize that teaching is a demanding craft. Give teachers some slack, but hold them accountable for doing the right thing for and with your child.

178.

Don't be fooled into thinking that the teacher with the most college degrees is necessarily the best teacher. Natural talent is a part of good teaching that can't be taught in graduate school. Go with the teacher whom the kids like most *and* who gets the best results.

179.

Stay out of teachers' faces. (Teachers don't like to be smothered any more than students do.)

180.

Never be afraid to ask for a second opinion. If you question a particular diagnosis, evaluation, or placement of your child, dare to request a review. Misdiagnoses can happen in education, just as they do in medicine.

181.

Get to know as many school staff members as possible (not just teachers). You can't have too many allies. Sometimes, help comes from unexpected sources.

182.

Don't try to tell your child's teacher how to teach. If you want to control how your child is taught, try home schooling.

183.

Get involved in parent organizations (PTA, booster clubs, etc.). Don't just join—be active. You can't expect parent groups to fight your individual battles for you; but you can count on them to provide parenting information, raise funds for worthwhile school programs, promote child safety and welfare, and work for school improvements.

184.

Don't be intimidated by school personnel. Parents are just as important as teachers and administrators in determining a child's school success.

185.

Pay attention to the paper blizzard sent home from school. It's not just junk mail. Papers sent home often contain information about important options, opportunities, and activities for your child. Don't let your child miss deadlines or miss out just because you didn't notice.

186.

If you have a choice, pick the toughest teacher, not necessarily the most popular.

187.

Never miss a parent-teacher conference. (Both parents should attend if possible.) It's easy. It's free. It's fun. And it's too good a deal to miss out on.

188.

Make the most of every parent-teacher conference:

- Have a goal.
- Write down questions in advance.
- Be prepared to share information about your child.
- Take notes for future reference.

189.

At conference time, bring up your issues first so there is time to deal with them. Don't allow your concerns to become the last-minute topic. Your agenda is as important as the teacher's.

190.

Show up for parent-teacher conferences early. You may be able to steal a few extra minutes with your child's teacher. If not, you may still use the time to examine your child's work and compare it with the work of others.

191.

If a teacher conference is likely to be particularly tense or sensitive, suggest meeting on neutral ground. How about a neighborhood coffeehouse or fast-food joint?

192.

If something doesn't feel right about what's going on at school, check it out. Trust your instincts.

193.

Always share with your child what the teachers say at conference time or any time. Silence or secrecy feels like a conspiracy to a child.

194.

If you have concerns, don't wait until the next formal conference period to discuss them. Request a conference whenever there's a need. Your child's feelings and progress should never be put "on hold."

195.

Be sure you fully understand your school's report card. Some are full of jargon and confusing symbolism. You don't want to miss or misinterpret something important.

196.

If your child isn't making as much progress in reading as you think is appropriate, it's time to talk to the teacher and come up with a plan. Keep in mind, however, that there's a difference between getting more help and just putting more pressure on a child.

197.

If you don't understand why your child isn't succeeding at school, ask the tough questions and persist until you get real answers.

198.

Keep in weekly contact with your child's teacher(s) whenever grades fall below a C.

199.

Don't blame the school for your mistakes.

200.

Take time to try to see the teacher's side of things. You and your child aren't always right.

201.

When necessary, be a squeaky wheel. Your child's learning deserves as much grease as anyone's.

202.

Exercise reasonable patience. Allow time for school programs or corrective action to work.

203.

If you have complaints, learn the "proper
art of bitching" to school personnel:

- ▓ Get all the facts.
- ▓ Follow established channels.
- ▓ Be specific.
- ▓ Avoid personal attacks.
- ▓ Be sure it's your child's problem, not
  just your own.
- ▓ Don't bully. It doesn't work with
  professionals.
- ▓ Time your complaint. (Friday
  afternoon is not a good time to
  air a gripe.)
- ▓ Leave the door open for future talks.
- ▓ Buffer your child from any conflict.

204.

If you have to go to the principal:

- Make an appointment. (Don't just barge in.)
- Both parents should go if possible. (If not, bring along a friend for moral support.)
- Don't be combative.
- Be prepared. (Use facts, not hearsay.)
- Be polite. (Civility works.)
- Dress appropriately.
- Understand that principals protect teachers but are usually open to compromise.
- Take notes.
- Arrange for some kind of follow-up.

205.

Want a child's final grade changed?
Think twice before you try. Realize it will
be difficult (maybe impossible) and will
alienate school personnel. Pursue a grade
change only if you're sure a profound
injustice has occurred or you have some
other compelling reason for not allowing
the grade to stand. If you decide to go
ahead, here are the steps to take:

1. Be prepared to progress up the
   ladder (teacher, principal,
   superintendent, school board).
2. Put your request in writing.
3. Dare to harass. (Call weekly.)
4. Consider radical measures (e.g.,
   contact the media, talk about
   running for the school board over
   the issue, mention an educational
   malpractice suit, hire a lawyer).
5. Persist.

206.

If the school calls, return the call ASAP. Your child's schooling isn't an I'll-get-back-to-you-when-it's-convenient deal.

207.

If you have to present your case to the principal, superintendent, or school board, you can increase odds of a favorable reception by finding out how they like to receive information (e.g., written form, oral presentations, statistical data, graphics). The appropriate secretary can tell you. (Good secretaries know everything.)

208.

Don't bad-mouth any teacher, course, activity, or program without thinking. It may turn out to be your child's favorite.

209.

Read the teacher's comments on your child's schoolwork. They're put there for a reason.

210.

Know when you are over-involved in the school and your child's learning. There's a difference between support and suffocation.

211.

Get to know your child's teachers as human beings. Learn about their likes, dislikes, and hot buttons. The more you know about teachers, the easier it is to figure out what pleases, satisfies, tickles, and impresses them.

212.

Teachers over thirty don't like to be shocked. Advise your teenager to avoid flaunting exotic tattoos or body parts pierced in unusual places.

213.

If the teacher won't answer your phone calls, don't tell the principal. Tell the office secretary. She'll get results without any fuss or hard feelings.

214.

Don't even think about kidding your
child's teachers about suing them. (It's
like joking about a bomb in an airport.)
The number one fear of today's teachers
is being sued by parents. They worry
more about potential litigation than
about being fired, discipline problems,
insufficient time, or lack of support
(results of 1999 survey by the
Association of Texas Professional
Educators).

215.

Double your impact. In all dealings with
school officials, approach them as a
couple whenever possible. Two parents
or guardians always have more clout
than one alone.

216.

Support merit bonuses or added recognition for outstanding teachers. Today, the best teachers don't always make the most money. Schools pay for graduate courses and advanced college degrees. This practice rewards those who are the best students, not necessarily the best teachers.

217.

If you're a noncustodial parent, request that the school send you copies of your child's progress reports and other important documents. (Provide self-addressed envelopes if necessary.) You can't help if you are out of the loop.

218.

Don't hesitate to check your child's
school records if you think they might
contain false or misleading information.
You have the right to review the file
anytime and to correct or rebut any
errors or misleading entries. Your child's
past records can affect decisions about
your child's future, including college
admission.

219.

Urge your school to create a parent
resource center offering one-stop
shopping for parents looking for
pointers, answers, guidance, and peer
support. It only makes sense that the
school help parents find what they need
to help their children succeed.

220.

Always send a note of appreciation to your child's teacher at the end of the year, even if you have to be creative to think of something to appreciate. Teachers share impressions of kids and parents. It never hurts to have a reputation as a pro-teacher family.

221.

Get to know the superintendent of schools. Friends in high places are very useful.

222.

If your school has a site council or parent advisory committee, get on it if you can. It's another way to help shape your child's education.

223.

Encourage your children to visit last year's teachers to share how well they are doing in the next grade. It will make both the teachers and your children proud.

224.

Spoil the good teachers. Give them extra encouragement, support, and recognition. Your child can't have school success without them.

6

Helping with Homework and Study Skills

225.

Homework is part of the deal. Allow for it. Plan on it. Show your child that even grown-ups have homework sometimes.

226.

Don't expect your child to learn exactly the same way you did. There is no single right or wrong way to acquire knowledge and master new skills. Whatever works is the best approach.

227.

Guilt diminishes people, rather than motivating them. It never works on the job, in the family, or at school. Don't use guilt on your child, your child's teacher, or yourself.

228.

Don't let an IQ score (or any score) become a self-fulfilling prophecy for your son or daughter. Natural ability can be stretched by

- exposure to varied experiences
- exposure to situations that build on existing strengths
- exposure to praise and reinforcement for genuine accomplishments—even little ones

229.

Pamper your children and give them a little extra slack during the first few weeks of school. This is always a stressful time for kids.

230.

Insist that your child get some phonics training. Period.

231.

Display academic work (math papers, spelling tests, etc.)—not just artwork—on the coveted refrigerator door. It sends a subtle message about what's important.

232.

When furnishing your child's study area, pay attention to ergonomics. Select a chair that provides proper lower-back support, and choose a desk with the right height to permit working naturally without undue physical discomfort, stress, or strain.

233.

Never make your child do homework as a punishment. It's intended as an assigned opportunity, not a penalty.

234.

Admonish your child to stop complaining about schoolwork and just do it. Whining accomplishes nothing, turns other people off, and makes the complainer feel worse. Time and energy spent complaining can be better used to actually get something done.

235.

Never use humiliation to get your child to study harder. It won't work. You'll get better results by showing your child respect.

236.

When talking to your children about schoolwork, listen to yourself. Often, kids hear more from your tone of voice than from your words. Avoid patronizing or sermonizing.

237.

Don't bargain or make deals to get your kid to do homework. Instead, provide support, encouragement, or recognition for work well-done.

238.

Resist the urge to over-intervene when your child is doing homework. Have trust and confidence in your child's ability to learn independently.

239.

Avoid power struggles over homework.
They're almost always lose-lose
situations.

240.

How about giving your child a monthly
book allowance (money that can only
be spent on books of your child's
choosing)?

241.

Provide a united front. Both parents
should agree on homework expectations
and rules. If kids see any wiggle room,
they'll wiggle by manipulating one
parent against the other. Stand together
and stand tough.

242.

Help your children get the map habit. A good way to start is by locating the place names they hear on the evening news.

243.

If you pack your child's lunch, stick in a reminder of after-school appointments or which books are needed for homework. A note of encouragement might be a welcome day-brightener for your child, too.

244.

Read everything your children read (storybooks and textbooks), and talk about what you read. It makes your children feel that their reading is important.

245.

Encourage your children to space their homework over the entire weekend. If everything is put off until Sunday night, it may not get completed. When students start off behind on Monday morning, they never seem to catch up all week long.

246.

When they're ready, have your children read to you. It's even more powerful than reading to them.

247.

Don't expect every lesson to be learned the first time. Good teachers and good parents know the value of patience.

248.

Have a no-interruption rule during homework time.

249.

Many parents save their children's good school papers. Why not try saving a few of your child's bad papers as well? They can be valuable later on to show how much improvement has occurred. All kids like to see how far they have come. It motivates them to keep working.

250.

Don't hover. Monitoring homework doesn't mean constantly looking over your child's shoulder. Back off. Checking in at regular intervals is enough.

251.

Invest in a magnetic poetry set. The kids
(and adults) in your household will have
fun practicing their writing skills by
rearranging the magnetic words to
create their own poems on the family
refrigerator.

252.

Point out spelling errors whenever you
see them in signs, menus, ads, church
bulletins, etc. Kids need to know that
someone notices. Maybe we can make
the next generation better spellers.

253.

Encourage your children to use a "buddy
system" so friends can remind each other
of homework assignments and due dates.

254.

When helping your child review and recite the multiplication tables, try doing it with the lights out. Something about the dark intensifies concentration.

255.

Laminate your child's important school pictures and papers that will be handled a lot or displayed at school for a period of time. This added touch of class can distinguish your child's work.

256.

Talk to your children about how each one learns best. Help them experiment with different study and learning techniques at home in order to sort out what works best at school.

257.

Once you understand your child's prevailing learning style (natural way of learning), discuss it with the teacher. Shared information is the only kind that works.

258.

Don't do your children's homework for them, but help when needed. Your most important role is to be there to cheer your children on.

259.

Try to get the families on your block to agree to a common homework time. That way, the neighbor kids won't be tempting your child to come out and play during study time and vice versa.

260.

Sometimes, it's hard to get kids to start on homework. Sometimes, it can be even harder to get them to stop. Set an upper limit (quitting time) for homework. A good night's rest is important, too.

261.

When your child has to memorize information for school, these student-tested techniques can help:

- Tape-record the information and have your child listen to it during downtime (e.g., while riding, waiting, or just hanging out).
- Write the information on cards and hide them around the house where your child can't help encountering them unexpectedly.

262.

Help your child understand that the time to start studying for a test isn't the night before the exam.

263.

Don't feel that you always have to have the answer. Kids learn best when they have to find their own solutions.

264.

The excitement of science lies in conducting experiments. You can't have a science lab in your home, but you can buy a few basic science supplies and a book of simple experiments for children. Turn your budding scientists loose. Dare to let them make a mess. If science isn't fun, children won't buy into it.

265.

Keep a log of the books your child reads and rank them with a five-star rating system. The log will be useful for choosing books for younger siblings. Better yet, if all parents share their five-star picks, everyone's kids can benefit.

266.

Pay attention to inattention. A young child who is constantly fidgeting, hyperactive, and inattentive may suffer from ADD (attention deficit disorder). If you suspect a problem, check it out.

267.

Kids inherit math phobia from grown-ups. Show your kids that math can be fun.

268.

Be sure your children have the four essential homework helpers: (1) an age-appropriate dictionary, (2) an up-to-date atlas, (3) a user-friendly thesaurus, and (4) a copy of the current year's almanac. (Of course, all of the information in these sources can also be found on the Internet, but your children can't curl up on the sofa with the Internet or take it with them wherever they go.)

269.

Limit your child's TV viewing on school nights to two hours. That's right—two hours! (The national average for kids is twenty-one hours and fifty-nine minutes per week, according to a recent NEA survey.)

270.

Watching TV isn't bad. Watching bad TV is bad. Turn your child on to the good TV available on the Learning Channel, the History Channel, or other educational channels. Learning and entertainment can mix.

271.

Work with other parents to set guidelines for such issues as TV viewing, Internet use, alcohol-free parties, and working hours for minors. When parents present a united front, things go better for everyone at home and at school.

272.

Keep a family project box containing paper, scissors, glue, markers, a ruler, a stapler, and other supplies needed for those special homework assignments kids always forget until the last minute.

273.

Let your children correct your spelling, grammar, and math errors. This way you both grow a little.

274.

Manage TV use in your family. TV is a robber of time and can contribute to antisocial behavior. The National Association for Education of Young People (NAEYP) cites three negative effects of watching too much TV violence: (1) desensitization to others' pains, (2) increased fear of the world, and (3) increased aggression. The NAEYP suggests parents watch TV with their children, make rules and expectations clear, resist putting a TV set in their children's room, and examine their own TV use.

275.

Make friends with retired teachers. They're great resources for after-hours homework help.

276.

Use time-tested, popular family games to boost learning skills. Yahtzee helps increase math prowess, and Scrabble is a great vocabulary builder.

277.

Always check to ensure that homework is done and done correctly. Nine out of ten teachers say parents don't do enough of this.

278.

Introduce your child to crossword puzzles. They're lifelong vocabulary-builders.

279.

If you expect it to be quiet in your child's homework area during study time, it should be quiet in the rest of the house as well. Parents and siblings should respect the quiet rule, too. After all, homework is a team sport.

280.

Help your children start their own filing systems at home. It's never too early to start relying on files, not piles.

281.

Take inventory of how your family spends time. You may be surprised. Most families don't use it the way they think they do. You can find time for "family time"—and homework, too.

282.

Encourage journal writing. It helps young people blow off steam, clarify feelings, and improve writing skills at the same time.

283.

Kids aren't scared of science unless grown-ups make them so. To children, science is just organized curiosity. Your attitude toward science is contagious. Have fun with science with your child.

284.

Don't put off helping your children overcome procrastination. Teach them to allow extra time, set realistic goals, make lists, and check off completed tasks.

285.

Butcher paper and poster board—these are two things students often need for school projects and presentations. Yet, few families have them around. Keep some on hand. Your child just might be impressed with your preparedness.

286.

Help your child get and stay organized. Organization is one of life's survival skills. Using an indexed notebook for assignments is a good way to start.

287.

Never be embarrassed about hiring a tutor for your child. (In Japan, it's a way of life.) Think of the tutor as a personal trainer for your child's mind.

288.

Get your child interested in current events. Read the newspaper and watch TV newscasts together. Talk about what's happening around the world and across the street.

289.

If your kids hate math, give them practice keeping bowling scores, balancing a checkbook, figuring batting averages, and computing gas mileage. When kids see that math is life, they often try harder.

290.

Encourage your children to select science fair projects based on their interests, not on yours.

291.

It's time for a tutor when
- grades are plummeting
- the teacher recommends it
- the child asks for it
- there has been an extended absence
- the student is moving to a new
  school with a different curriculum

292.

Take your time finding the right tutor,
just as you would when selecting a good
mechanic. "Fixing" your child is a lot
more important than repairing your car.

293.

Don't rush to judge or correct your
children. Give them room to bloom.

294.

Sometimes, the best tutor for your child may not be a human being. Consider employing your family computer as your child's tutor. Software is now available for all levels of learning, from reading readiness to preparation for college entrance exams. Go ahead and let your computer help boost your child's school success.

295.

Know the difference between a tutor and a mentor. A tutor helps build skills and increase knowledge. A mentor fosters wisdom, wonder, insight, and passion for living and learning. Your child may need both. They could be you.

296.

Don't bluff. If you don't know the answer to a homework question, don't guess or make one up just to help your child finish an assignment. If you don't know, say so and find the right answer together.

297.

Textbooks are full of tools that go unused. Chapter reviews, thought questions, and extension activities are put there for a reason, but most students ignore them. Urge your child to take advantage of all the text offers. It's another small way to get ahead of others.

298.

If your school, library, or community has a Junior Great Books program, get your child involved. Never pass up an opportunity to connect children with reading and good literature.

299.

Make a big deal out of makeup assignments. Know your school's policy on makeup work. Get assignments in advance of an absence if possible. Don't let your child fall behind by default.

300.

A day without homework is a good day to make up past assignments or get the jump on future ones. (Of course, a day off now and then isn't all bad either.)

301.

Start your child learning a foreign language as early as possible. Better yet, learn together. Foreign language proficiency will be a passport to college and career opportunities later on.

302.

When your children are old enough, give them a copy of *The Dictionary of Cultural Literacy* by E. D. Hirsch, Jr., et al. It's full of common references everyone should know as part of our cultural heritage. This "dictionary" is a valuable resource for understanding history and literature and can enrich your child's writing.

303.

Be sure your children have all of their completed homework when leaving for school each day. Perfect work left at home is still late. As the popular credit card ad says, "Don't leave home without it."

304.

You have to understand your children to help them. Know what they take to show-and-tell and why. It's a peek into what's important in their lives.

305.

Nurture the author in your young child. Encourage writing without fussing too much over spelling or grammar. That can come later.

306.

If you have a reward system for school achievement, reward improvement— not just top grades. Progress, not perfection, is about all any parent should expect. Improvement is success. It deserves a payoff.

307.

Is it worthwhile to have your child recopy a messy paper? You bet. Neatness is never a mistake. It's a sign of success at all levels.

308.

Allow your children to educate you. Let them show you what today's teachers want and how they want it. Sometimes, children know best. Get used to it.

309.

Check your child's handwriting speed. The average writing speed varies from 45 letters per minute (LPM) at fourth grade to 67 LPM by sixth grade. Some kids try so hard for picture-perfect letters that they write too slowly to keep up when taking notes. If your child is significantly off the mark, have him or her consciously practice writing faster.

310.

Encourage your kids to spend the last five minutes before bedtime reviewing what's coming up the next day and double-checking their preparation. They will gain the sense of control necessary to succeed.

311.

Try putting a fountain or an aquarium in your child's study area. The calming effect can reduce distractions and make it easier for your child to focus.

312.

Resist urgings to write your children's papers and book reports for them. It's cheating. Worst of all, it cheats them out of the chance to learn how to do it themselves.

313.

Urge your child to do the most distasteful assignments first. Delaying never makes such assignments easier or more pleasant.

314.

Most public libraries have terrific summer reading programs for young people, often featuring incentives, rewards, and special events. Get your children to take advantage of them. If there isn't time for relaxed reading during the summer months, your family is missing the whole point of summertime.

315.

Give your children a good planning
calendar and show them how to use it.
A calendar is a tool successful students
use to ensure that important schoolwork
gets done on time every time.

316.

Enroll your child in a mail-order book-
of-the-month club for kids. There's
something special about getting a
book in the mail. It gives your child
something to look forward to and
provides a monthly boost to your
child's interest in self-directed reading.

317.

If you bring work home, don't cloister yourself in your home office to get it done. Instead, do it at the kitchen table alongside your kids doing their schoolwork. When homework is a family affair, kids think it's a natural way of living and learning.

318.

Encourage your kids to trade good fiction books with friends just as they exchange baseball cards.

319.

Enlist neighbors to share their expertise by serving as homework helpers, whom students can call when they need help.

320.

Sports teams hold training camp before the regular season starts. Why don't students and families? Try holding a short "review, drill, and practice camp" for your children right before school opens. A running start builds confidence and impresses teachers.

321.

Give your child an edge by sharing these proven test-taking techniques:

- Skim the entire test before starting.
- Answer the easiest questions first.
- Never leave multiple-choice questions blank.
- Outline all essay answers.
- Review all answers before handing in the test.

322.

Try having your child sign a homework contract committing him or her to study for a certain amount of time each day. Kids are impressed by documents they have to sign.

323.

Help your child learn geography. Follow family trips on a road map. Point out on a globe where important world events are happening. Anything that helps kids understand their place in the world helps them do better in school as well.

324.

In school, as in life, tackle the big stuff first. This is a lesson that both parents and kids need to learn.

325.

Who says you can't have spelling tests in the summertime? Working on a short word list each week during the summer can give your child a leg up when school starts.

326.

If the teacher allows students to retake tests to improve their grades, encourage your child to take one of these offers (unless there's a good chance your child will do worse the second time). Merely caring enough to try again impresses teachers.

327.

Tip your child off that assignments turned in early stand out. Papers and projects submitted with the rest of the pack get their share of attention and no more. Early assignments receive special attention. (Of course, late assignments get noticed too—but the effect is entirely different.)

328.

Learn to understand your child's standardized test scores. They're not gibberish. These scores pinpoint your child's strengths and weaknesses. Scores are tools for building school success if you know how to use them.

329.

Book clubs are reclaiming popularity. Why not a family book club? Have your family take time once a month to discuss what you have been reading individually and collectively. It will help make your children more eager readers and your family a more interesting place to be.

330.

Know the signs of an underachiever:

- resists homework
- forgets assignments
- daydreams frequently
- manipulates teachers and parents
- practices creative excuse-making
- cons others into doing his or her work

If this sounds like your child, it's time to put on a little parental pressure.

331.

Rote learning is out of fashion, but some things are still worth memorizing. Teach your child that memorizing is easier when spread over several study sessions, rather than crammed into one memorizing marathon.

332.

Music has a lot in common with math. Learning Latin increases understanding of English. Help your child see the connections between subjects. Schooling makes more sense that way.

333.

Periodically have your children fill out a report card on themselves. It always pays to ask, "How am I doing?"

334.

Advise your children not to loan their
class notes or homework to anyone.
They might not get their work back, and
they could be enabling a cheater as well.

335.

If your child is diagnosed with a learning
disability, point out that he or she is in
pretty good company, including Albert
Einstein, Tom Cruise, and Cher.

336.

Toss out the clock. Homework goes
better with no clock in the room.
Watching the clock doesn't make the
time or the work go any faster or slower.
It just doesn't go at all.

337.

Unplug the phone. Many families have success limiting phone use during study time to calls about homework assignments.

338.

Convince your children that they can still get good grades in physical education even if they are uncoordinated and unathletic. The secret is to show up, be in uniform, take a shower, participate, and have a good attitude. That's all it takes.

339.

If getting your child to complete homework assignments is a chronic problem, consider hiring a high school or college student as a "homework coach." It may work better than your constant nagging.

340.

College fraternities and sororities have always made good use of test and term paper files. Families can too. Keep your older child's schoolwork as a resource for younger siblings. Saved schoolwork offers clues about what teachers like, what works, what doesn't, and what errors get noticed most.

341.

Urge your older children to do what successful business leaders do. Use downtime to dispose of mundane tasks. The time kids spend "on hold" or waiting can be used to check off onerous assignments that don't require much thought.

342.

Don't just accept that your child "isn't good at math" or "doesn't have a way with words." Many students do poorly in some subjects because they (and their parents) give up too soon. Most students can do satisfactory work or better in *all* subjects. Get extra help, spend more time—do whatever it takes to get your child up to snuff. Don't let mediocrity happen by default.

343.

When your kids have to write an essay for school, be sure they include the three basic components—introduction, body, and conclusion—and that they have a summarizing statement in there somewhere.

344.

To help your children remember more of what they study, have them try these memory helps:

1. visualize what they read
2. think of examples
3. categorize and organize information in their minds
4. use rhymes to recall isolated facts

345.

Help your children discover the power of three-by-five cards. They're perfect as flash cards for reviewing math tables, vocabulary words, and algebraic or physics formulas.

346.

When working together on reading or math skills, pay attention to when your child begins to get tired, bored, frustrated, or distracted. It's best to quit while it's still fun.

347.

Encourage your child to worry less and work more. Worry, guilt, regret, and self-doubt waste time that could be better spent studying.

348.

When tackling long-term learning projects, encourage your child to make a checklist of all the steps and when each step needs to be completed. Checking items off is fun and provides intrinsic motivation to keep going.

349.

If your children enter a science fair, be sure they understand that their projects will probably be rated on clarity of purpose, research techniques, findings, conclusions, use of visuals, overall presentation, and clarity of written work. It's hard to win if you don't know how the judges keep score.

350.

Use the dictionary as a coffee table book in your house. Make it a habit for family members to look up and share the new words they encounter during the day— every day. This makes vocabulary-building a family project.

351.

If your children are in a homework rut, have them vary their routines. Do homework before dinner or after dinner. Whatever is different. Change the order in which they do assignments. A fresh approach can be energizing. It's always better to get out of a rut than to dig it deeper.

352.

Be patient when quizzing or helping your children review subject matter. One of the biggest mistakes parents make is to rush to fill in any awkward pauses. Allow enough time for your child to come up with the answers. Teachers call it "wait time."

353.

Give your child this simple checklist for proofreading written compositions:

- The paper says what the writer intended.
- Every sentence is a complete thought.
- All sentences start with a capital letter and end with punctuation.
- Spelling is correct.
- Paragraphs are indented.

354.

If your child ruins an important project or assignment, don't pooh-pooh the incident or try to be philosophical. The problem may not be important in your world, but it is in your child's. It won't help to explain that it's just one event out of a lifetime of school experiences. As one student said, "That's easy for you to say. You're all grown-up already."

355.

If you want your child to be a good writer, make writing a part of everyday life. Write notes to each other. Write letters to friends and relatives. Let your kids see you compose E-mail messages. In families where writing is a natural and necessary means of communication, kids write more and write better.

356.

When your child loves a movie, urge him or her to read the book the film is based on. The book is often better. This is another way to sustain or rekindle your child's interest in reading.

357.

Just because a child is absent from school doesn't mean that his or her homework can't be present and accounted for. When your children miss school, fax their homework assignments to their teachers. It's another way to demonstrate conscientiousness.

358.

If the teacher indicates a specific length for an assigned theme or essay, have your child try to come as close as possible to the suggested word count. Anything less is viewed as an incomplete assignment. Anything more is a minor source of irritation for the teacher.

359.

Math is more important than ever in the new millennium. Do whatever you can to urge, encourage, coax, or cajole your child to take algebra, geometry, and calculus in high school.

360.

Help your child lead a balanced life. Make time for more than school. "Homeworkaholism" has nothing to do with school success. Academic achievement isn't measured by the number of hours studied, but by results. Living a well-rounded life is a secret of sustained school success.

361.

As your children mature, they should be able to spend more "time on task." Observe how long they study or work on homework without a break. If the time on task isn't increasing as expected, use a timer and make a game of consciously stretching the time between breaks.

362.

Can a kid study too much? Absolutely! If schoolwork is driving everything else away, encourage your child to lighten up, take a lesser grade if necessary, and get a life. School success isn't just being successful on paper. It means being successful in living as well.

363.

Help your children match the difficulty of library books to their ability levels. The five-finger test can help. Have your child read a page out loud. Hold up one finger for each mistake or unknown word. If you end up holding up five or more fingers for a single page, the book is probably too difficult.

364.

Insist that your child make a backup disk of all schoolwork done on the computer. You don't want the experience of trying to console a child whose long-term project suddenly disappeared because the computer crashed.

365.

What if the dog really does eat your child's homework (or some other far-fetched mishap causes completed homework to be lost or destroyed)? If the incident really is implausible but true, *you* tell the teacher. Don't make your child be the bearer of lame tales. The teacher might think your child is lying but may believe an adult's version.

366.

Encourage your child to be a peer tutor. There's no better way to learn than to help others learn.

367.

Point out to your child the lessons to be learned from their daily school and life experiences. The experience is wasted if nothing is learned. As Archibald MacLeish said, "There is only one thing more powerful than learning from experience and that is not learning from experience."

368.

Some families allow their children an hour of TV viewing for every hour spent reading. Think about it.

369.

If nothing else works, dare to allow your child to fail a test, a course, or even a grade level. Sometimes it takes finding out what failure feels like to really learn what's important, how to succeed, and the true meaning of consequences.

370.

Be sure your kids understand that they work to get good grades for themselves and for their future—not for you. It can change their attitudes toward studying.

7

More Family-Tested Ways to Boost School Success

371.

Be sure your child goes to school every day. Showing up is the first step to success.

372.

Get as many caring adults involved in your child's education as possible. The more people who care, the harder it is for your child not to.

373.

Be sure your child has at least one hero or heroine who is an outspoken fanatic in favor of education. It could be a master teacher. Better yet, it could be you.

374.

Talk to your child about what happened at school—*every day*. Ask open-ended questions. Don't accept "yes," "no," or "nuthin'" as satisfactory answers.

375.

Let your child in on what teachers like and dislike:

Like	*Dislike*
Smiles	Rudeness
Cleanliness	Whining
Courtesy	Profanity
Neat work	Back talk
Taking turns	Showing off
Turning stuff in on time	Gross behavior

376.

The best time to find out what happened at school is just as soon as your child arrives home. If possible, sit down right away and let your child unload. You'll get more spontaneous information then than any amount of dinner-table interrogation will reveal hours later.

377.

Location is everything. Check to be sure your child is seated in the classroom where he or she can see and hear all instructions.

378.

Buy your child a stapler. It's a good
answer to the problem of lost or
separated papers. An assignment that
can't be found or has pages missing is no
better than an assignment never done.

379.

Pay attention to what your local school
board is doing. Its decisions can impact
your child. If pending board action will
adversely affect your kids, let your views
be known by writing or calling board
members, leaving a message in the
board's voice-mail box, or attending a
board meeting. Most school board
meetings now have an "open mike"
portion for public concerns.

380.

Some families have a special school bulletin board for all school-related calendars, reminders, announcements, and notices. It's an easy way for everyone to keep up with what's going on. Think about it.

381.

Provide your child with hands-on history experiences. Visit historic sites and reenactments of historical events. History comes alive when kids actually walk the battlefields and see firsthand where and how things happened.

382.

Be your best when your child is having his or her worst day.

383.

If your child's teacher uses cooperative
learning in the classroom, be sure your
child doesn't get stuck doing all the
work, or doesn't let someone else do it
all. The idea is that everyone pitches in
and everyone learns.

384.

Don't be conned by your kids. Don't
believe everything they tell you about
what teachers do and allow in school.

385.

Encourage your children to compete
with themselves. (Keeping charts and
graphs can help.) That way, they
always win.

386.

Involve grandparents in your child's schooling. They're a built-in booster club.

387.

Help your children survive a bad teacher by

- learning on their own (giving themselves assignments)
- reading independently
- making the most of computer learning software
- doing extra-credit assignments
- developing hobbies and outside interests
- looking to other learning resources such as libraries, music lessons, and club activities

388.

Don't panic if your child doesn't blow the top off an IQ test. Keep looking. Your child will have strengths in other areas. There's more to school success than a lofty IQ score.

389.

"Catch-22": spend at least twenty-two minutes of uninterrupted, full-attention time with each child every day. It doesn't sound like much, but it's a lot more than the national average of thirty minutes a week. Even if you don't see the connection with school success, your child will.

390.

Be sure your children know their rights and responsibilities. When all parties live up to their sides of the bargain, school success is a piece of cake.

391.

Network with other parents. You can help each other raise successful learners. That's the right way to keep up with the Joneses.

392.

Take time to hear out your children when they tell you about their schoolday. When kids are cut off, they feel that what they do isn't important.

393.

Tell your child how much you enjoyed school, but don't make it sound like you were always successful. Your child shouldn't have to live up to the perfect example you never were.

394.

Teach your child how to shift gears in reading. Not all material should be read at the same speed or with the same intensity.

395.

Keep your perspective. If your child gets one bad grade, it's not the end of the world. Take grades for what they are. Many letter grades are more subjective than objective. Some are just guesses.

396.

If your child doesn't want to go to school some morning(s), resist the temptation to give in. Try to find out why, but don't back down. Explain that adults have to go to work every day and kids have to go to school every day. It's not negotiable. It's their job.

397.

Pay attention to your child's complaints about school, but don't encourage whining.

398.

Let your child learn about your job. Show how you use what you learned in school. A little real-world motivation never hurts.

399.

Make it a point to attend every school
event, game, or performance your child
is involved in. Being there shows you
care and that what your child does is
important. If you can't attend, arrange
for a close friend or relative to substitute
for you. Every kid deserves a fan in
the stands.

400.

Show pride in your child's school. Wear
the school colors. It's another sign you
support your child's learning.

401.

Praise effort and reward achievement,
but don't base your child's learning
on bribery.

402.

If your child won't tell you what's going on at school, volunteer to drive the car pool. You'll get an earful.

403.

If your child believes that a lucky charm helps to do well on tests, don't argue; but insist on some solid preparation as well.

404.

Schools give kids a fresh start. Parents should too. Allow your children to succeed all over again or to start over—whatever fits. Sometimes a clean slate is the best gift you can give to a learner.

405.

Advise your children not to volunteer that they didn't study when they happen to get a high grade. Why blow a good image?

406.

It always pays to know what to expect. Talk to parents of students who were in your child's teacher's classroom last year. If you know what's coming up, you can help your child prepare for it.

407.

If your child needs to turn things around, consider summer camp. Many kids reinvent themselves while away at camp.

408.

Most city libraries have an information department that will find the answer to almost any question over the phone. Encourage your child to use this service. It's a fast, painless way to conduct research and more reliable than the Internet.

409.

In your eagerness to have your child succeed in school, don't try to make your child into someone he or she isn't. Work with what's there. As business writer Marcus Buckingham suggests, "People don't change that much. Don't waste time trying to put in what's left out. Try to draw out what's left in. That's hard enough."

410.

Try not to let your personal problems (e.g., divorce, job loss, bankruptcy, depression) interfere with your children's learning. Buffer them from your worries by assuring them that your problem is not their fault, making clear that they are not responsible for finding a solution, reaffirming your unconditional love, and reassuring them it's going to be OK.

411.

The sixth grade is often a pivotal year for girls. Cliques and peer relationships can crowd out other concerns, and schoolwork may suffer. It's hard for girls to succeed academically when they feel left out socially. Help your daughter weather this sensitive period by reaffirming her strengths, helping her understand puberty's physical changes, and allowing latitude in dress and accessories so she fits in.

412.

Don't push your child into too many activities. Exposure to varied experiences helps learners, but too many can overwhelm them. If you're stressed out by too many demands, don't pass it on to your child. Break the cycle.

413.

If you want all your children to succeed in school, avoid favoritism. Support all equally. Treat all alike—fairly.

414.

Read the school's student and parent handbooks together with your child. That way, you each realize that you both know how things are supposed to work.

415.

Urge your children to include visuals and graphics (e.g., drawings, photographs, diagrams, graphs, charts) in their oral and written reports. (One picture is worth . . . well, you know.)

416.

If your child is adopted, don't go out of your way to let people know. Even today some teachers and administrators will rush to blame adoption for every school problem, instead of looking for real causes.

417.

Teach your child to pay attention to personal hygiene and good grooming. These things shouldn't affect grades, but sometimes they do. Would you give an unkempt student with bad body odor the benefit of the doubt after being cooped up together in a stuffy classroom all day?

418.

If you suspect that your child is intercepting mail from the school, ask the office to send pupil progress reports and other important information in plain envelopes not bearing the school's letterhead or logo.

419.

Your child may be in over his or her head (i.e., placed in the wrong grade) if your child

- associates mostly with younger children
- doesn't finish assignments
- daydreams a lot
- spends a lot of time stalling (e.g., sharpening pencils)

420.

Keep a scorecard of your child's past school successes. Sometimes, you have to remind kids of the good times in order to keep them motivated during the bad times.

421.

Don't treat gifted children with kid gloves. Just treat them like children. Gifted kids should be no more exempt from doing chores, behaving respectfully, or being disciplined than anyone else. The biggest problem gifted students have is feeling "weird and different." Don't reinforce that feeling.

422.

If your child absolutely has to remember to take something to school the next day, don't take any chances: place it right by the front door, tape a note on the bathroom mirror, and pin a reminder on the student's backpack.

423.

Hobbies can teach valuable skills that carry over into schoolwork. If you want your children to have a hobby that teaches a sense of timing, requires ongoing practice, involves self-discipline, improves coordination, provides an immediate sense of accomplishment, builds performance skills, and is fun, introduce them to magic.

424.

If your child is missing a lot of school due to a prolonged illness, arrange (bribe if necessary) for a friend from your child's class to drop by to give your child a daily briefing. It will keep your child up-to-date and feeling connected. Maybe the teacher would be willing to come by occasionally, too, if you ask.

425.

Should a busy student be excused from chores at home? Maybe sometimes; usually not. Parents are also busy, but they have to hold up their end at home. Kids should, too. That way they learn responsibility, another requirement for school success.

426.

Some families coordinate their summer vacations with what their kids will be studying during the coming year. If the kids are going to study the Revolutionary War, the family may vacation in Boston, Lexington, and Concord. If the curriculum calls for studying outer space, the family may visit NASA headquarters or the Kennedy Space Center in Florida. Think about it.

427.

Don't let your student become too smug over past achievements. It's always possible to do better. "The biggest room anywhere is the room for improvement." (Harvey MacKay)

428.

What to do about cheating?
1. Be clear about your own values.
2. Discuss what ethical behavior means to your family.
3. Don't look the other way.
4. Don't buffer your child from the consequences of cheating.

429.

Make it a house rule: "We don't settle for half-hearted effort."

430.

Be a cheerleader for your children on the playing field or in the classroom—especially when they're losing.

431.

Some students and families celebrate the end of the school year. Why not celebrate the beginning? It's a time of new clothes, new books, new teachers, and new opportunities. Try a back-to-school party. It will send a message that education is important and school is fun.

432.

If your school doesn't have a Parent Communication Network (PCN), start one. It's one way parents can work together to share information, agree on common standards, and prevent kids from scamming them.

433.

If your child changes schools or moves to a different town, monitor new friendships closely. Troubled kids gravitate to newcomers; new students, eager for friendships, respond to any overture. Unhealthy friendships are easy to come by. A bad start with the wrong friends can cripple learning. Find ways to connect your child with the best and brightest students in the new setting.

434.

Encourage your children to create their own momentum by forcing themselves to get started and taking advantage of good moods.

435.

Encourage your child's constructive use of discretionary time. Research shows that kids who spend seven or more hours a week in positive activities do better in school and get in less trouble than those who spend a lot of time with friends "with nothing special to do." Examples of constructive time use include music lessons, sports, clubs, volunteering, and church or synagogue activities.

436.

Help your children understand that part of learning is discomfort. Doing nothing is comfortable. Trying and risking are not.

437.

Encourage your children to apply a reality check to their educational and life goals. The old saying still rings true. You can have *anything* you want; but you can't have *everything* you want.

438.

Help your child build a little serenity into each day. Mother Teresa taught us that "God is a friend of silence." Our noisy world drains us, but a little quietude can be an elixir to help us press on. Even little kids need quiet time.

439.

Don't typecast your children (e.g., "he's only an average student" or "she's not very good in science"). Let your children show you who they are. They'll surprise you.

440.

Feelings drive performance. How your child feels about self, school, family, and life in general determines his or her effort, enthusiasm, and persistence. Listen for the feelings behind your child's words.

441.

If your child is gifted, resist the urge to push too hard, to steer your child into early specialization, or to pressure your child to devote full-time to studies. "Better to ease up on the pressure so a gifted ten-year-old has some chance for a life after thirty-five." (Paul Kropp)

442.

Talk to your children about the four common thinking traps:

1. hasty thinking (impulsiveness)
2. narrow thinking (biased or provincial assumptions)
3. fuzzy thinking (impreciseness)
4. shotgun thinking (scatterbrainedness)

Without thinking about it, many students fall into these traps. Encourage your children to think about how they're thinking.

443.

Never try to motivate your child with negative verbal put-downs. They can devastate a child's self-esteem. Some of the most damaging comments are "Why are you so stupid?" and "You'll never amount to anything." The absolute worst thing a parent can say to a child is "I wish you were never born."

444.

Spring fever can undermine an otherwise successful semester. The last few weeks of school count as much as the first few weeks—sometimes more. Urge your child not to quit too soon. (It's not over until it's over.) Finish strong. If you ever use inducements or incentives to keep your child on task, the last month of school may be the time.

445.

At the end of the school year, pause with your child to review the past term. What worked? What didn't? What should be done differently next year? It will give you both closure for one year and set the tone for the coming one.

446.

Pass on to your children Marian Wright Edelman's "lessons for life" from *The Measure of Our Success*:

- Never give up.
- Don't ever stop learning.
- Don't fear hard work.
- Choose friends carefully.
- Finish what you start.

447.

Think of your children during the day. Send positive mental vibes in their direction. It just might give them an added boost. Stranger things have happened.

448.

Some communities are now organizing Day 1 programs whereby adult volunteers personally welcome all students back to school and plan other special surprises for the first day of the new school year. The purpose is to show kids that they are special, that the community supports them, and that school is important. How about trying this in your community?

449.

Sooner or later, kids need to test their wings, make their own mistakes, solve their own problems, and figure things out for themselves. Grit your teeth and do nothing if that's what it takes to help your children succeed in school—on their own!

450.

Your child's worst day at school is just that—a day. There will be other, better days. Be sure your child understands that.

Special Ways to Help Preteens and Adolescent Learners Succeed in School

451.

The best defenses against eroding school success during the crucial middle years are to show your love (life is too short to keep affection a secret), model a healthy lifestyle, stay involved in your child's life, and talk openly about teenage issues.

452.

Before the first day of middle school, arrange for your child to practice opening the lock on his or her locker. It's amazing how many capable and competent preteens are terrified by a simple combination lock.

453.

What's the most powerful threat parents
can make to a middle school student
who misbehaves in class and gets bad
grades because of it? Most teachers say
it's "If you don't shape up, I'll come to
school and sit with you in every class."
If parents say it and mean it, results are
virtually guaranteed.

454.

Early-adolescent girls often begin
doubting their abilities. Parents can
help their daughters sustain, retain, or
regain self-confidence. Stress ability.
Downplay appearance. Involve your
daughter in sports. Support special
talents and interests. Encourage a
can-do attitude.

455.

Dare to keep track of where your adolescent children are, who they're with, and what they're doing. It's not being nosy. It's called parenting.

456.

Stay put. If you possibly can, avoid moving during your child's middle or high school years. If there is ever a time to put family first, this is it.

457.

Pay attention. Resist denial. If your preteen or teenager is losing weight, losing friends, or losing out at school, something's wrong. Find out what and start setting it straight.

458.

To keep your middle school student on track,

- hang in there (endurance is important in parenting)
- stick to your values
- lighten up on lesser issues (don't wage war over trifles)
- address problems head-on

459.

With the escalation of negative pressures, influences, and temptations during the preteen and teenage years, this is the time to stand tall with your child. Parents are the adults in the equation of adolescence. Act like one.

460.

Don't let your adolescent children narrow their interests too soon. Help them to keep their options open and to look for multiple possibilities.

461.

Don't waste too much time worrying about how hard it is for teenagers to grow up today. It's supposed to be hard. Tough challenges and hard choices promote growth.

462.

If your child needs a pep talk to spur greater effort at school, call on a favorite coach to help. Coaches are good at pep talks, and kids listen to them.

463.

Have you heard about the National League of Junior Cotillions? It's a nonprofit program that teaches preteens and teenagers manners, etiquette, dance steps, and social skills. Students who feel comfortable and confident in social situations do better in school. Cotillion is well-established in the South and gaining popularity in the North. Check it out.

464.

Follow the three Cs when setting boundaries for middle and high schoolers. To be effective with teenagers, limits should be *clear*, *concise*, and *consistent*.

465.

Don't make more of your children's athletic accomplishments than you do their academic achievements.

466.

The biggest distraction from schoolwork for teenage boys isn't girls. It's the automobile. Thinking about a car, saving for a car, choosing a car, supporting a car, showing off a car, and working on a car can become an obsession. Set car-use rules and limits early on and stick to them.

467.

Make plans, not excuses, for your teenager.

468.

The best way for a teenager to learn to like science and math is to take a course in the subject—and succeed. Don't allow your children to slip through high school never trying what they think they don't like.

469.

Can a student succeed in both sports and academics? Yes—*but*. Your children can be successful as students and athletes, but they will have to apply the self-discipline they learn on the playing field to the classroom as well. It's your job to see they understand it takes extra effort to be a winner in sports *and* academics; but it's worth it.

470.

Learn the latest teenage slanguage. Not to be cool, but to understand what your kids are talking about. You can't help them if you don't speak their language.

471.

Don't let your teenager get in the habit of using stimulants to stay awake to study. Stimulants are fickle and can be addictive. If students are excited about what they're learning, adrenaline is the greatest stimulant of all.

472.

Realize that being cool is a survival skill for teenagers. It may explain some changes in demeanor and attitude toward school.

473.

Make sure that your high school student takes academically challenging courses. Anything less is a cop out. A transcript of good grades in easy courses is just a track record of mediocrity. Colleges and employers can spot students who seek the easy way. They're looking for something better.

474.

Limit the hours your teenager works at an outside job. Many counselors recommend no more than fifteen to twenty hours per week. Don't let a job interfere with schoolwork or attendance. School is still your child's number one job.

475.

Make friends with your child's high school counselors. They know the ropes about career choices, college entrance, financial aid, and a lot more.

476.

Stay connected with your high school student. It's a myth that teenagers don't want or need parental involvement.

477.

Know what classes your teenager is taking and who the teachers are. It's called involvement. Anything less is like not knowing who your spouse works for.

478.

Some behaviors can bring your adolescent's schooling to a sudden halt. Taking weapons to school or making terroristic threats are unacceptable in today's society. Be sure your teenagers understand that these acts are out of bounds and can put them out of the game for good.

479.

Make sure your high schooler gets enough sleep. Teenagers are notorious for sleeping in class. Unfortunately, in school, as in life, "you snooze— you lose."

480.

Try to schedule your teenager's hardest subjects at mid-morning. Adolescent metabolism isn't always ready for calculus at 7:30 A.M. but is raring to go by 9 or 10 A.M.

481.

Be sure your child understands the academic eligibility requirements for participating in sports.

482.

Watch for the seven signs of student alcohol or drug abuse:

1. changes at home (e.g., withdrawal, anger)
2. changes at school (e.g., new friends, truancy)
3. changes in appearance (e.g., dark eye circles, poor grooming)
4. changes in lifestyle (e.g., secrecy, unexplained cash)
5. changes in personality (e.g., mood swings, paranoia)
6. use of cover-ups (e.g., incense, eyewash)
7. physical evidence (e.g., pipes, roach clips)

483.

If you don't know how to talk to your teenager about school problems or at-risk behaviors (e.g., drugs, sex), tell them so. That's a start. Build from there.

484.

Get acquainted with your middle and high school organizational chart. Find out who does what in the school's front office (e.g., Who handles attendance? Who's in charge of discipline?).

485.

Support any school activity your teenager is interested in. It may not be your favorite, but it is helping him or her feel connected. It may even be all that's keeping your kid in school.

486.

Monitor your teenager's school
attendance religiously. Give the school
all your work, voice mail, emergency,
unlisted, and beeper phone numbers.
Pay attention to attendance figures on
report cards. It's like balancing a
checkbook. Your figures should
reconcile with the school's.

487.

Don't let your adolescent even think
about dropping out of school. Kids
don't have to love school. They do have
to cope with it, work within the system,
get what they can from it, and use it as a
means to an end. In our society, there
are few rewards for abandoning
schooling.

488.

If your teenager develops a negative attitude that school "sucks," consider these actions:

- Talk to the school counselor.
- Reevaluate expectations and parental pressures.
- Change teachers or courses.
- Lighten your teenager's load.
- Explore alternative programs.
- Try setting short-term goals.
- Don't give up.

489.

Don't let your daughter use the menstrual cycle as a con (e.g., faking cramps) to get out of physical education class. It's the number one gripe of middle and high school physical education teachers.

490.

Appearance shouldn't count so much in school, but it can. Encourage your teenagers to "costume" themselves as normal learners—not freaks, terrorists, or rebels without a cause.

491.

Don't dictate your teenager's college choice, but don't be a silent partner either. Your wisdom, wishes, and wallet count for something.

492.

Start your teenager's college search and visitations as early as the sophomore year. Major life decisions take time.

493.

If college entrance exam scores are a concern, get help. Legitimate coaching programs are available. Look under "Tutoring" in the Yellow Pages. Gains of fifteen to thirty points are not uncommon.

494.

Explain to your child the importance of completing a college application correctly, completely, and carefully. The application is an extension of the student. It should show his or her best side. These tips can help: read all instructions, run an extra copy for use as a rough draft, and pay strict attention to deadlines.

495.

Give your teenager some practical advice for surviving the first crucial year of college, such as

- get a good advisor
- join a study group
- practice moderation in alcohol use
- associate with good students
- remember why you're there

496.

The key to helping your kid get started at college is . . . *relax*. Help move in, say a cheerful good-bye, and leave.

9

Final Words

497.

Doing all the right things to boost school success is hard. Doing all the wrong things is easy. Here's a surefire recipe for promoting your child's failure in school:

- Use threats and intimidation.
- Adopt a judgmental attitude.
- Punish mistakes.
- Withhold affection.

498.

The final test of school success is life. You'll know you've done a good job when your child begins worrying about boosting your grandchild's school success.

499.

Encourage your adult children to keep on learning throughout life. "What happens is that most people declare themselves 'done' when their formal education is over. What is it about renting a cap and gown and a scroll of paper that makes us think our learning days are over?" (Peter McWilliams and John-Roger McWilliams in *Life 101*)

500.

Never stop boosting your child's learning success. The only difference is that, as you and your child mature, your role shifts from directing and decision making to modeling and influencing.

501.

Only one thing is better than watching your children grow, learn, and keep trying new things at every age: doing it yourself.